An Elegant Echo

An Elegant Echo

Answering Your Negative Thought Patterns with Positive Affirmations

C. J. Hoffman

iUniverse, Inc.
New York   Bloomington

An Elegant Echo
Answering Your Negative Thought Patterns with Positive Affirmations

iUniverse books may be ordered through booksellers or by contacting:

iUniverse
1663 Liberty Drive
Bloomington, IN 47403
www.iuniverse.com
1-800-Authors (1-800-288-4677)

ISBN: 978-1-4502-2615-8 (pbk)
ISBN: 978-1-4502-2617-2 (ebk)

Printed in the United States of America

iUniverse rev. date: 6/18/2010

The Joy Reminder, Inside the Honey Walls, and now the final book in this series of mind tools 101, *An Elegant Echo,* are finally completed. I extend my humblest gratitude to my dedicated readers and those who have encouraged me to be better in what I do, especially the editors at iUniverse, who have shown me a glimpse of what it means to convey my ideas through the written word. My blessings go out to all of you as you live the life that you were meant to enjoy.

C. J. Hoffman

Contents

Introduction

An Elegant Echo is first of all a book of stories, for if nothing else I am a storyteller. Many of the stories written in these ten chapters are true-life experiences that I wrote in the form of parables, using real scenarios from my forty-plus years of counseling experience. Other times the account that I have to tell is better served as an intimate story, and I take great care in doing that. I use these two approaches to writing in order to engage you in a personal one-on-one "life trek" that may precipitate and end in the enjoyment and clarity in your everyday life that you richly deserve.

As we explore *An Elegant Echo* together, I encourage you to read each story and then follow through by further investigating with me the value of the life lesson contained in it. Each unique story or parable in this book describes a process where you accept, or have accepted in the past, words that are said to you with high emotion and dramatic experiences instilled in you as your truth.

Very often, genuine experiences that your subconscious mind considers valid, your conscious mind takes for granted to be true. You will learn in *An Elegant Echo* that the subconscious mind never lies, but it does not always tell the truth. The subconscious only deals in bare facts. It does not substantiate the truth or falsehood contained in those facts.

The word "elegant," as it is applied in the title, means "clever" or "inventive." It refers to your subconscious mind where every word or situation is indelibly incised and then stowed. Those words and experiences are stored in your subconscious mind exactly as you heard or experienced them. Every taste, smell, crash you heard, sunburn you felt, episode you encountered—negative or positive, and your reaction to those stimuli—are all there. They are crammed into your subconscious mind like sardines in a can, just waiting for the appropriate trigger to slither out into your conscious mind and cause confusion in your thought processes.

As you learn more about your subconscious mind, you will notice that it is rather dense, it does not edit anything that it takes in, and it cannot discern truth from fiction. Your subconscious mind actually believes everything that it tells your conscious mind because it knows no better.

In time and with practice, you will learn to cover your own subconscious negative positions, and you will master the process of overlaying that negative position with a more positive one. I cannot say that you will be able to erase that negative thought or experience from your subconscious mind, but you will be able to overlay it and, in time, you will become so adept at doing this you will hardly be able to give the negative position room to grow or influence your conscious mind.

As you engage in reading the ten chapters of *An Elegant Echo*, you will find that the knowledge that you gain will cause you to become more aware of your own "mind speak" so that a real change can happen in your life. I enjoin you to practice the few simple steps that I outline after each story. They are there to assist you in changing your negative mind-set to a positive one using the mind tool that I suggest for you. You may want to undertake this process in order to implement positive changes in your conscious mind. I promise that when you change the way you think, you can readily notice a remarkable difference in the way you live your life.

In *An Elegant Echo*, I write about imprints. Imprints, as they are used here, are the words, thoughts, and experiences that occur in everyone's life. I truly believe that no one escapes the faultless harassment of the subconscious mind.

In your childhood, when many imprints are carved into your subconscious mind, you are innocent and defenseless against them. As a child you are sensitive to new words and experiences, especially those words that are said in anger and those experiences that punish you physically or emotionally.

A small group of stories, sprinkled throughout *An Elegant Echo*, speak to the occurrence of childhood imprints. I have written them so that you can think about whether something similar happened to you. Maybe you feel there is no hope for relief from the negative thoughts in your mind's cycles. That is not even close to the truth, as you will soon realize.

The second group of stories included in *An Elegant Echo* will shepherd you through instances of imprinting that may occur during the young adult period of your life. This frequently happens when you build upon those negative words and situations that are already imprinted in your subconscious mind as children. Those additions that you construct could create some miserably unhealthy situations during your adult life. The triggers for your subconscious imprints actually compound the effect of negative thought on the way you are able to live your life as a daughter, son, father, or mother.

When you search for those instances of amplification, imprint built upon imprint, you will become infinitely more aware of the effect they have on your quality of life. When you become aware of your established pattern of building upon your imprints, you are better able to do something about them.

The third group of stories reflects those instances of negative thought that imprint your mind in your senior years. As a senior you recognize what your major imprints are and possibly feel that nothing can be done to alleviate the contrary effects of those long-standing negative thoughts and experiences. Furthermore, you feel that you are immune to the possibility that you could acquire even more imprints in your later years.

Consider the fact, then, that no matter when your subconscious inclines its ear and absorbs words or experiences of the negative kind, I can teach you to overlay those imprints. Note that any time a negative thought comes to your mind unbidden, you can do something about it. You will learn how to do it as you read each story and parable in *An Elegant Echo*.

All the stories and parables in *An Elegant Echo* were written to illustrate the negative imprint that could affect you. Each chapter is set up so that you can read the story first. Some of my readers stop there, but I encourage you to read further—through the story and on to the **Mission** section of each chapter. This section will clarify the subject of the story, and it serves as a bridge to the information that is addressed in the ensuing section titled **Execution of the Process.**

The instruction for the conversion and overlay of negative imprints is found in bullet form in the **Execution of the Process** portion of each chapter. This thought-provoking part of your exploration will show you how to determine what part of that lesson resonates with you. It will illustrate just one way to overlay the negative imprint with the positive imprint. The way you effect this result is by the use of a mind tool, the affirmation.

This affirmation is a positive statement that you learn to compose for the express purpose of changing your mind from the negative to the positive. It is a most natural tool for you to use, because when you talk to yourself (using the affirmation) you are able to convince your conscious mind that what you say is true while overlaying the negative imprint of the subconscious mind.

In the final lesson of each chapter, you will discover the **Classic Lines** component. Most of these versions of the truth stated in the story are authored by famous writers, statesmen, or philosophers. It is here that I draw on some of my all-time favorite pieces of literature and poetry for you to enjoy, think about, and perhaps make a part of your own personal philosophy.

I want to encourage you here to value each of your imprints and keep them strong, positive, and healthy. The practice of positive affirmation can change your life if you decide to invest the time in becoming the person you know that you can be. As an added incentive, you will be left with the awareness of the difference between the negative and the positive imprints, and that you can make those changes to your own mind, which will bring you joy. I wish you peace and happiness as you begin reading *An Elegant Echo*.

Chapter 1:
Marvin the Poor Soul

I attended Sara's rather beautiful wedding one Saturday in spring many years ago. My most vivid memory of the ceremony is that the groom kissed his new bride on the forehead at the end of it.

At the reception the ladies at my table chatted about how beautiful the gowns were, how spectacular the flowers were, and oh yes, the music was absolutely celestial. No one cared to address the hippo sitting in the middle of the table.

Even though we thought the groom's actions a bit bizarre, we made a silent pact by rolling our eyes and giving sidelong glances, so as not to judge the young man. And we shrugged the whole thing off as we toasted the happy couple.

Fast-forward nine years: One day in early summer, I received a phone call from Sara, and we made an appointment for a counseling session the following day. The subject of the session was to be her marriage.

If you were a guest at Sara's wedding and you were as curious as I was, you knew there was a back story about that kiss. You were sure that this appointment with Sara was on the horizon from the very beginning of her marriage and that, sooner or later, Sara would require the services of a counselor.

Sara arrived for her appointment already upset and in tears. I ignored the tears and instead asked her if she would like something to drink. She nodded and hiccupped in the affirmative.

I walked to the kitchen to get her some ice water, opened the cabinet, chose a pretty glass from the highest shelf, and filled it with icy spring water from a pitcher brought out from the refrigerator. I took my time walking back to the living room where I had left Sara. That bit of benevolent neglect gave her time and space to pull herself together, and she accepted the water I proffered with a much brighter "Thank you."

I was always gratified when a few moments alone dried up a woman's tears and resulted in a better frame of mind. And for a man who was desperate, that same bit of benign neglect would take his testosterone level down a few notches with the same results.

Sara began her sad story at the altar of the church where she was married, and she was prepared to bring me up-to-date by telling me every detail of her life with Marvin, her husband. She remembered every part of it like it happened yesterday, because she cycled those negative thoughts over and over in her mind for years especially that kiss.

When I mentioned the kiss, she confessed that she was very confused by her husband's odd behavior at the end of the wedding ceremony, but she decided not to address it during the reception. But after the reception, and as they rode off together on their way to their honeymoon in Canada, Sara discovered to her horror that she didn't need to question Marvin about the kiss. Marvin volunteered the answer to the question that she didn't have a chance to ask. Sara remembered that it was so well thought out and smoothly spoken to her that Marvin must have rehearsed it for some time before he devastated her with it.

According to Sara, the reason Marvin kissed her on the forehead on her wedding day was that Kathy, the woman Marvin really loved, had attended the ceremony. Marvin hadn't wanted to hurt Kathy's feelings, and when he was faced with giving Sara a real kiss, he decided on the forehead instead of the lips.

I was stunned by her story—so much so that for once I could not think of a thing to say except that I was very, very sorry.

How had Marvin kept this woman he really loved a secret while he dated Sara for two years and was engaged to her for two more before they married? Furthermore, how could he be so cruel as to apprise her of his plan after the wedding and as they were embarking on what should have been precious time together? I had so many questions, but I ignored the niggling in my mind to ask them as Sara continued—because that was not the end of her story.

Marvin further outlined what their married life would be like. He would visit Kathy twice a week for sexual relations. He and Sara would have sex until she became pregnant and had the child. After the birth of the child, they would do it all over again until she had borne him three children. After Sara had raised their children to school age, she would no longer be needed. She would leave their home, their children, and Marvin's life so that he could marry the woman whom he really loved.

Marvin hatched this grandiose scheme because Kathy couldn't bear children and Marvin wanted children. Now I needed a drink, but I was not sure that what I craved was water.

I finally stopped Sara well into her long litany of hurts and grievances, because I felt that I could be of help to her with the information that she had already given me. And I had heard enough about Marvin to last me for the rest of my life.

I asked Sara to put down the empty water glass that she was still clutching and to sit back in her chair, close her eyes, and relax. After a few moments, I quietly questioned her about what she was hearing in her mind. "What are the words that keep going round and round in your brain?"

At first, she could not detect any discernable words or phrases, but as she relaxed for the second time against the back of the blue wingback chair, she sighed. A good sign, I thought, that she was ready to listen for the words.

Suddenly she sat upright, with eyes wide open, and screamed again and again, "You always leave me. You always leave me."

I stood and slowly walked to her chair, knowing that her glazed eyes were not taking notice of me but were experiencing some far-removed trauma. I touched her shoulder, and she reacted with a start, just as if she had awakened from a nightmare, still shaking but in touch with reality.

After a few moments of quiet conversation, I was able to glean from her disjointed rambling that she had witnessed an experience in her childhood that had become a negative imprint. Sara had felt abandoned by her father, and the negative imprint became an amplified imprint when Marvin cruelly acquainted her with his idea of the way their marriage would play out. At the end of the marriage, when she was no longer needed to raise their children, Marvin convinced her that she would not only be abandoned by him but by those three children as well.

The imprint was no longer a neat one-story imprint. Thanks to the odd situation she found herself in with Marvin, it had developed into a skyscraper sized negative imprint.

I leaned over and held Sara in my arms. She was sobbing by that time, and I felt that she needed to grieve that negative imprint of abandonment before we went any further. When we were both exhausted from the emotion, she moved from her chair to the couch. Sara put her feet up on the soft cushions, as I suggested, and accepted a small pillow for under her head. She quickly fell asleep. I gently covered her with a soft blanket from the hall closet, crossed the room to my own chair, and briefly nodded off.

Sara did not awaken until early evening, and when she sat up, the first thing she did was check her watch and come to the conclusion that she must rush home. She had to have dinner on the table by six o'clock sharp. That was one of Marvin's rules.

Sara hurriedly promised to return the following afternoon. We said our good-byes with a hug, and she walked quickly out the door, across the porch, and down the front steps. The last thing I heard as I slowly closed the door was the *click, click* of her heels as she strode up the sidewalk to her car.

The next day when Sara arrived, she had herself very together and walked in right on time. Marvin's rule: always be on time for appointments.

This time we headed to the kitchen for some freshly made iced tea.

On the kitchen table, I had placed some notes from our meeting the day before so that we could review them. But before we could do that, Sara snatched them away, tore them into tiny pieces, and dropped them back on the table. Sara had decided that she was just fine and didn't require a review of the previous appointment or any helpful instructions. She apologized for taking up my time and asked me not to mention our meetings to anyone, especially Marvin.

Many times as a counselor I think that my head may just explode and spatter brains all over the wall! Sara had come much too far to go backward now—but I recognized that all-encompassing fear that can come upon anyone when they can't visualize the road ahead. They may panic, going back the road they just walked because that road, although certainly not a smooth one, was a familiar one.

I knew from experience that there was no sense in trying to talk Sara out of the negative mind-set that she had developed overnight, so after she gave me a halfhearted hug and walked quickly from the kitchen, I just watched her as she went through the hall and out the front door, leaving it slightly ajar in her haste to leave. I had trouble getting Sara off my mind that night as I tossed in my bed trying to get comfortable.

In a few days, I received a whispered phone call from Sara—she must come to the manse immediately, and would I be there? She had not waited for my answer. She hung up and was on my back porch in minutes.

Mission

I did not mention the last time we spoke because I sensed that Sara had done a great deal of thinking since that time. I did reconstruct the notes she had previously shredded and put together a list of possible affirmative instructions for her to use in the healing process in which she was about to engage. I handed the results to her. Sara scanned the notes and the short list of suggested affirmations as I walked over to the stove to stir the large kettle of syrupy strawberry jam that was simmering there.

I was certain that the road ahead for Sara was going to be challenging, and overlaying this double-edged negative of abandonment was going to take a substantial commitment on her part, simply because Sara lived with Marvin. By his very proximity to her, he was a constant trigger for her abandonment issues.

Sara went immediately to work and chose two of the positive statements I had listed as possible affirmations, as her own. She decided that she wanted to use as her affirmation two short sentences: "I am never alone. God has my back."

The words and the sentiment were simple and calming, two attributes for an affirmation capable of changing Sara's mind. And she truly believed those statements she had chosen for herself, which was an additional plus.

Execution of the Process

Sara walked with me down the long hall from the kitchen to the front of the manse and across to the large mirror beside the front door. She took off her glasses and methodically placed them in her purse, giving herself time to develop the resolve that she needed to do the work that was ahead of her. Then she directed her gaze to her own eyes in the mirror, as I instructed her to do. She muttered her chosen words shyly at first, but after a few practice affirmations she declared them in a very clear and confident voice. I had never heard her speak in such a forceful manner and had never seen that look on her face. She slowly but powerfully repeated, "I am never alone. God has my back."

We said our good-byes that day with tears of happiness. We both knew that she had made a decision—a very powerful one—and was, at the very least, on the path to her recovery.

What a difference the constant and consistent overlay of those simple positive statements made in Sara's life. Here are the instructions that I gave to her and that I give to you if you have that sometimes terrifying negative imprint of abandonment:

- Write a few positive affirmations that resonate with you.

The affirmations must seem valid and true to your own personality.

- Find a mirror, any mirror—you can use a compact mirror if you have to.
- Engage your own eyes in the mirror. If you have trouble looking in your own eyes, you can take the following alternative route below.
- Raise your head so that you are looking almost into your eyes, but not quite.
- Repeat to yourself, "I love you."
- Every time you repeat the phrase "I love you," move your eyes closer to your eyes in the mirror, until you are gazing directly into them. I have concluded, after I witnessed this phenomenon multiple times, that if you do not love yourself, for whatever reason, you will have a difficult time making eye contact with your own eyes. When you follow the above process and you are serious about it, it will work for you. Why is it important to look yourself in the eyes? It becomes very important when you understand that it is the first step in the process of using the valuable mind tool of affirmation.
- Repeat the affirmations that you have chosen every time you pass a mirror.
- In Sara's case, I asked her to report back to me as often as she needed to do so—day or night. In your case, perhaps you have a friend or clergyman you are able to talk candidly with who will provide this needed support for you.

At first, Sara was careful not to let Marvin see or hear her practice her affirmations, but the fear quickly vanished as day after day she repeated her phrases into the mirror with growing confidence. You may have this same problem, but know that you will get over it.

I can't report that Sara was cured of the negative imprint of abandonment, but I was soon sure that the ogre of her abandonment issues was under her control and not the other way around. It is the same with everyone. The negativity in your subconscious mind will not be erased, never to return. But it will be overlaid with a positive affirmation, which in time will render the negative imprint void, as far as you are concerned. It cannot hurt you ever again if you stay aware of your own "mind speak."

Sara knew that something insane had happened to her on her wedding day, but she was so shocked by Marvin's idiotic strategy for their lives together—and apart—that she did not have the presence of mind to tell him that she was not up for his crazy plan and to leave the situation.

After a few months of practice and a few late-night phone calls that signaled what I called a "crisis of confidence," Sara experienced a complete turnaround. I was, and am, so proud of the work that she performed to bring about a positive change of mind for herself. In the year that followed, she became a strong, self-assured woman who was a role model for her three young girls.

Marvin had been moved to the background as far as Sara was concerned. He was nevertheless adamant about sticking to his original plan, which fact she ignored when he occasionally brought the subject up.

In the end, Sara's life became filled with the joy she thought she would never experience again. She finally had the courage to discount the marriage contract that she had never consented to in the first place. Sara gratefully learned to walk her own walk. And you will too.

Classic Lines

You may read this partial comment in a context extraneous from the one for which it was written, but it certainly could be likened to the sorry state of affairs between some men and women today: "… Everywhere you see widows whose husbands are still alive." This was written to Pope Eugenius III, during the Second Crusade in 1146 AD.

Chapter 2:
The Guitar

Gene had already learned the power of overlaying the negative imprint with the positive affirmation, since he had visited me previously with a problem for which he had no difficulty identifying the negative imprint. It was a problem most of us suffer from: speaking in public. He no longer felt negative emotion from that imprint as he assumed the role of teaching the gospel to a large church in Oregon. Simply because he did the work of overlaying that particular negative imprint with his positive affirmation, he was able to fulfill a lifelong ambition to serve in the capacity of a pastor.

But still, the negative imprint was sometimes triggered when he arose to speak in an unfamiliar venue, such as a much larger church on the East Coast. Gene heard this "mind speak," but it no longer held negative emotion for him, signaling that he was set free from the bondage of that particular negative imprint.

When he arrived at my front door not long ago, Gene was suffering from a new and debilitating negative imprint that he was having some difficulty identifying. He sat down across from me and calmly related these two stories:

One day a few weeks before he came to me, Gene determined that once and for all he would learn to use the family computer. He pulled his chair up to the desk that held the dreaded computer and tried to stare it down. When that didn't work, and as his fear was multiplying, he just sat there in front of it, humiliated. He was so paralyzed with fear that he was unable to place his fingers on the keyboard.

Gene, as most of us do, wanted to learn to use the computer; in fact, he felt that he needed to use it because his young children were already far ahead of him in the process of mastering it. But he was frozen in place, powerless to begin, and he gave up trying because he couldn't function and didn't know the reason for it.

The second story Gene told me was that since he was a little boy, he had wanted to learn to play the guitar. And not long ago, he began once again the ritual that he had mastered without thinking because he had done it so many times before. He departed for the music store with his list of requirements to learn to play his beloved instrument. On that list were bullets that reminded him to choose a beginner's guitar and to select an elementary lesson book—one that taught all the rudiments of learning to play that guitar, a few picks, and two packs of strings, just in case he mangled some and they shredded as before, whipping around his head in a dangerous arc.

Now you would have thought that from all the similar trips he had made to Robbins Music store, he would have had all the necessary equipment at hand. But no, he had given all of it away time after time when he felt defeated and had given up learning the instrument.

After Gene leafed through the beginner's book and scanned the lesson plans, he felt confident that he could teach himself how to play the guitar from that beginner's book of lessons. So he bought it.

Gene thought perhaps visualization would help him this time around to finally complete this first lesson book. And the image he conjured up in his mind's eye was that of him, seated with the guitar in the correct position across the front of his body. He heard in his imagination the pleasing sound that the guitar made as he softly strummed it. Then Gene bought an expensive professional guitar instead of another beginner's instrument as further insurance that he would continue with his self-assigned project.

When Gene arrived home, he was so excited about his new beginning that he hadn't consciously remembered how he got there. He backed up the driveway, stopped the car, opened the door, got out, and ran around to the trunk to retrieve the beginner's guitar book and his new professional guitar in its black leather case. Gene almost forgot the small bag of guitar picks and strings that the salesperson insisted that he include in his purchase.

The door to the trunk was creaky and bounced back twice before Gene was able to firmly slam it shut. And as he juggled his purchases on the way to the front door, he searched his left pocket for his front door key. Finally he found it, turned the latch, opened the door, and stepped in.

He piled all his purchased treasures on the dining room table and returned to the hall to close the door that was still gaping open, removed his jacket, and hung it up in the coat closet.

The dining room table was a great place to learn to play the instrument, and he suddenly realized how quiet it was in the house before the children arrived home from school. Gene was thankful that he still had about thirty minutes alone until they did.

Eagerly he unclasped the guitar case, opened it, and picked the instrument from its red velvet resting place. The centerpiece on the table was just the right height to serve as a music stand for the lesson book, and he turned a few pages before he found the very first lesson. That page guaranteed that he would be playing a simple tune on his guitar before the hour was up. But where was the page that taught the novice how to tune the instrument? He leafed to the front of the book, nothing. He leafed ahead of the first lesson, but that didn't make much sense to him, and he started to perspire. Gene became flustered for the first time in a very long time.

Gene said that the first thing that popped into his mind frightened him, and he went into his study to calm down.

And what was the first thing to pop into his mind? It was "You are stupid."

Who do you think sent him that negative thought? Did someone whisper it to him from across the room, or did someone scream it loudly at him in anger a long time ago?

Wherever it came from and whenever he received this imprint is probably a moot point. The important thing to remember here is that Gene finally came up with the negative imprint that was preventing him from learning anything new and fencing off that part of his life that would give him joy. It was his subconscious mind that caught those words thoughtlessly spoken to him—that he was too stupid to learn anything. And it was the subconscious mind that saved those words for just such an occasion as this.

Gene knew that his subconscious was not inherently wicked in bringing up this imprint; it merely took at face value what was said to him. It had not made a judgment whether the statement was true or the situation was a valid one; it just stored what was said to him and played it back to him word for word. And it was always right. He had experienced those words at one time or another. Sometimes your conscious mind remembers when it happened and sometimes it does not.

Mission

Now let's address the trigger, the reason Gene's subconscious brought this negative imprint forward to his conscious mind in the first place. It was simply because he voiced his desire to learn to play the guitar. And because of that negative imprint, embedded in his subconscious mind that he was stupid, his conscious mind tried to warn him away from trying to learn anything new. It knew that it was painful to hear those words of failure the first time someone screamed them at Gene, and it did not want him to repeat that experience. He could have tried to learn a new dance or a new way to swing a golf club; it wouldn't have mattered. The subconscious mind would have triggered the negative thought that he could not learn or that he was stupid.

Now that Gene was sure of the identity of the negative imprint that prevented him from learning, he set about taking care of the negative emotion that it transferred to his conscious mind. He remembered the procedure that he had used to overlay the previous negative imprint and how to accomplish it, which made the composition of a new affirmation for this new negative imprint much easier. And he chose the affirmation "I am persistent."

The subconscious would not have discerned by itself what it should or should not have believed was the truth. It was a bit dull and accepted everything that it experienced—good, bad, or inane. It was not able to overlay the negative with the positive statement of its own accord, and Gene could not have merely insisted that the negative imprint go away. It was lodged forever in his subconscious mind as part of his life story.

Execution of the Process

This is where your conscious mind can be trained to intervene in the argument between your conscious mind and your subconscious mind.

You may begin with the choice of an affirmation to overlay the negative thought. Clearly map out what you want to say to your subconscious about your situation. You may want to say that, in your experience, you can learn anything that you really want to learn.

I will choose one affirmation for you for the sake of this lesson. And it is this: "No one and nothing can deter me." To make this affirmation effective, please do the following:

- Go to your mirror and think of the negative imprint that has been tripping you up.
- Look into your eyes in the mirror, and just as if you were speaking in anger to another person, loudly and with as much emotion as you can muster, proclaim to those eyes in the mirror the positive statement, "No one and nothing will deter me."
- As many times a day as you think of doing this, go to your mirror and repeat the exact same phrase with the same

hard-edged, loud proclamation. The more you practice this affirmation, the shorter the time will be that you will have to put up with the negative emotion that you feel about this imprint.

- Now you may feel silly the first couple of times that you shout into the mirror, but as you make some headway into laying the positive affirmation over the negative imprint, it will no longer embarrass you.

Why must you use the mirror and why all the shouted exclamations? Why can't you just sit down on a comfortable chair, close your eyes, and meditate? That is very easy to explain, and I usually do not have to do it more than once because it makes so much sense. The reason I instructed you to shout into your own eyes is that you most probably experienced the same situation when you were first imprinted with the negative thought that you were stupid. You saw a person shouting out, red-faced, saying how stupid you were, and when you saw it, you heard it, and your subconscious understood it and stored the words as an imprint.

If you used the process above, your subconscious saw, heard, and understood as well just how adamant you were to the contrary of that negative imprint. And your subconscious mind remembered the affirmation. Even though the negative words would come up again as you said your affirmation back to the negative thought, it seemed like your subconscious said, "Oh yeah, I remember that."

Please understand that every time you talk back in such a way to your subconscious, its grip on you lessens until you can smile at the negative words and ignore them if you wish. It is a great feeling to be free of the confines of just that one major negative imprint. It can open you up to a new and exciting life. There is nothing to cramp your style anymore as far as learning is concerned.

Classic Lines

This classic notation is one that will keep you thinking for some time to come. It is loaded. Be careful to think about it from all angles: "An intellectual is someone whose mind watches itself" (Albert Camus, *Carnets,* 1935–1942).

Chapter 3:
The Lie of the Hex

This story began on a farm in Enterline, Pennsylvania, where I spent a bit of time as a child. Our family farm was positioned smack in the middle of Dutch country with its rich culture and hardworking men, women, and children.

We learned quickly and clearly all the dos and don'ts that we were expected to be aware of if we considered ourselves members of the Dutch community. Of course, unless you were born there you were just kidding yourself if you believed that you would ever be accepted as one of them, but you could come close if you cared enough to try very hard.

My city-bred mother taught herself to "put up" all manner of vegetables, fruits, and meats, which she stored in handsome Mason jars in the corner of our stone-lined cellar. To my amazement the temperature below ground never increased to more than sixty degrees, even during the hottest of "dog days," but would decrease to a frosty forty-five degrees during the winter months when the jars of food took on an icy haze.

My city-bred dad learned by trial and error (mostly error) how to farm the fallow fields surrounding our house and outbuildings, but he had more success with chickens, geese, deer in season, and pork from his one lonely pig. Dad kept one stallion that he dearly loved but who had to be sold after a falling-out the two of them had about breaking out of the barn and destroying another farmer's field. That horse alone almost had our family excommunicated from the valley!

When I was young, I had no idea how poor we had become until one year when Christmas rolled around and there were no decorations, no tree, and no gifts. I remember that year because I felt fortunate that a boy in my class liked me. He liked me enough to ask his mother to help him choose a token of his esteem for me. Her gracious answer to this was to wash and press her prettiest hanky for him to wrap as a gift for me. I kept it for many years until I married, when it seemed to have gotten lost in the shuffle. I still occasionally think of the sheer white cotton background with tiny red roses printed on it and the dainty tatting the whole way around the little rolled hem. It was one of the best gifts I ever received because it expressed devotion and kindness from someone I hardly knew. I surely could have used that hanky a few times since then.

One experience that I do not hold dear was the hex. It all began when a neighbor's wife hailed down my school bus to hand me a note to give to my mother. We had lived among the Pennsylvania Dutch for a very short time and we were still wary of each other, but I did as she requested, as I had been taught by my grandparents.

I was very concerned, though, that I had done something that I was not supposed to or that there was something that I had not done that I was supposed to—I could not think which role I might have played, but I felt that I would somehow get punished because of this note. And I was right.

When I was dropped off late that afternoon at the farm owned by my school-bus driver, I still had about a mile to walk until I arrived at the edge of our property. It gave me a whole twenty minutes to think over the wisdom of actually delivering the note to my mother. I could lose it along the way or I could read it, and if it was something bad, I could tear it up and fling it to the four winds. And if I would have just done one of those two things, I could have saved all of us a lot of grief.

I soon found myself walking up the cracked cement walk. I hesitated before I carefully crossed the broken boards of the front porch and quietly opened, then closed, the kitchen door behind me. Maybe Mother was taking a nap or went into town for provisions—it was very quiet in the house, so it gave me a bit more time to think about the note.

Just as I sat down at the kitchen table and spread the now-wrinkled note as flat as I could on the table, my mother entered the kitchen and came over to where I was sitting before I could read it. She was holding her right hand to her forehead as if she was in severe pain. Underneath her hand were some pieces of ice wrapped in a dish cloth. She walked carefully, probably not wanting to jar the pain in her head. I handed her the note and said nothing. She opened the piece of yellow-lined paper and started to read it. Then she screamed something about Mrs. Dudry (the neighbor) as she tore the note into shreds and threw it on the worn linoleum floor in disgust. By this time I was up off my chair and holding onto her. She looked so ill that I was not sure that she would not break up into tiny pieces and fall to the floor along with that damned note. I was not allowed to cuss, but somehow this seemed to be the perfect time for it.

I was already punishing myself for giving Mother that folded piece of paper from Mrs. Dudry, when Dad came running across the yard from the chicken house carrying a few eggs in a basket. He dropped them on the kitchen floor after he took a look at his wife's face. He had heard her scream from across the yard, and while he took my place holding Mother together, I ushered my brother and sister, who had assembled for the same reason, outside to play to separate them from all the drama.

Later that evening when everything had calmed down, Dad pieced Mrs. Dudry's note back together enough to get the gist of it. Then he angrily pushed the note in my direction across the table where I was reading so that I could read it and understand what I had just done.

I could not understand why he was so angry with me since it was Mrs. Dudry who filled in the blanks of what I now would call a form letter. It makes me wonder just how many of these she wrote a week to have to resort to fill-in-the-blank format. As best I can remember it, the letter read something like this: "To Esther Hoffman (something about a hex put on her that morning). The indiscretion was: Esther had baked a chocolate cake with peanut butter icing on it (blah, blah, blah)."

She had given a piece of that cake to Mrs. Dudry's husband to eat while Mr. Hoffman was called from the lower fields so that Mr. Dudry could talk to him. Mr. Dudry had then returned home after he had his conversation with Mr. Hoffman and told Mrs. Dudry that Mrs. Hoffman's chocolate cake was the best that he had ever eaten—outshining her chocolate cake by a mile.

The postscript was that Mother should enjoy the headache that she would have until such time as our family moved out of the valley. You have heard it before, I know: you really cannot make this stuff up!

I guessed that clichés became clichés simply because they were true, because my family made use of another one and they "killed the messenger." I was punished for giving my mother the dreaded note from Mrs. Dudry, and the next week was spent indoors doing extra chores instead of going outside to run off some steam after school.

My mother got the worst of it, though. The headaches were almost more than she could take and even though she told us over and over that they had nothing to do with Mrs. Dudry's note, we did not believed her.

Mission

It is a difficult problem to solve when you have been hexed. Whether you believe in it or not, the results seem to be the same. Those wretched headaches would not let up.

It could be said that the headache that mother had experienced before she read the hex note from Mrs. Dudry was because the hex was initiated that morning, even though Mother had not received the note until five o'clock that same afternoon. Maybe Mother was right and the headache and the hex were not at all connected. But even at that young age I believed that there were cruel people, and just as we prayed to God for good things to happen, some people (fill in the name of Mrs. Dudry) prayed to the other side for rotten things to happen. To me, if you believed in the positive, the counterbalance was that you believed in the negative.

This eight-year-old child felt great sadness when she thought about Mrs. Dudry and because she felt so threatened by my mother. All my life, instead of blaming people for what they had said or done, I needed to know why they had said or done it. But soon after that, while I was in the throes of self-pity for being holed up in the house instead of running free, I came to this conclusion: I pitied my dad, who wanted so much to fit in with the Dutch community we found ourselves living in the middle of. Now he and his family were treated as pariahs, and he had this yellow-lined, pieced-together hex note to prove it. They wanted us to move out of the valley—at least Mrs. Dudry did.

When I reexamined this case for inclusion in *An Elegant Echo*, I discovered a few ways we could have looked at our problem in order to somehow right this wrong perpetrated on my mother and, through extension, my whole family. We could have forgiven the hex and ignored the hatred behind it. But then again, there was that blinding headache that would not go away and almost demanded that something be done about that fact. We could have turned the hex back on the perpetrator, saying, in effect, "backatcha."

I know now that the hard-core believers in such things have done that many times to each other! Back and forth they went with their threats until one of them either moved out of the community or died. But until either event came to pass, it was war. But we had done none of these things.

Mrs. Dudry had intimated in her "form letter" that my mother had some ulterior motive for being "hospitable" to Mr. Dudry, and this lie is the negative imprint I decided to capture for the sake of this lesson.

Just as almost everyone else in this world, I have been lied on and lied to, and so have you. Being lied to was not as difficult to deal with as being lied on. When you were lied to, usually you discovered all at once what the entire lie was when it was told to you. When you were lied on, the information seemed to have legs of its own and morphed out of control before you even heard about it. This may have caused anger, and further down the road, if you happen to have the negative imprint for it, your mind turned to self-pity.

Execution of the Process

This I would call a complex imprint, and it is not simple to eradicate—but it can be done. Again, I will take you to the solution to all of this by integrating your subconscious with your conscious mind through affirmations. You will use three affirmations to effect the change that is required to overlay the imprint of the lie in the hex, to overlay the imprint of anger (which we all know is really the other side of fear), and to overlay that aggravating self-pity.

- Choose an appropriate affirmation for your situation.
- Uncover all that you can about the lie that is being told about you in your own community.
- Write it all down on a piece of paper.
- Let's say for the sake of this lesson that you chose as your affirmation to cover the negative imprint of the lie, "I do not hold anyone responsible for the lie."
- Now for the second imprint that invariably screws itself into your subconscious in cases that involve a lie, anger.
- The affirmation chosen to cover the imprint of anger may simply be "It is smart to drop the angry thoughts."
- The negative imprint that we have left is probably the one that is most difficult to choose an affirmation for: self-pity.
- Deal with the self-pity with insight and understanding.
- Those questions that you bedevil yourself with about the why of the lie are of no consequence. You are full of self-pity from the telling of the story of the lie to yourself and

to others in your family, no matter what the reason that was told on you.

- Choose a phrase to cover this complex negative imprint of self-pity. The affirmation that I have chosen I have coupled with the first two phrases of the complex affirmation: "I do not hold anyone responsible for the lie. It is smart to let go of the anger. I let go of my self-pity." To some of you, this will sound like weakness on your part. It is anything but. To let go is difficult enough, but not to assign guilt is even more difficult. Furthermore, self-pity is more often than not a guilty pleasure, for we have a story to tell. Without that story, who would you be? You have to answer that question for yourself, but I know that you can take this liberating step on your way to change your mind for the positive.

- The repetition of the above complex affirmation should be performed in front of the mirror. The affirmation will be more effective when you can look into your own eyes to change your mind. Remember that practice is the key to making the affirmations work. Please do not plead no time available for the exercise of the affirmation, because it is very important to the way you live your life and how you interact with others. Of course you have the time!

Classic Lines

I found this very up-to-date piece the other day. An English poet wrote it in his poem, "The Progress of Error," in 1782. Celebrities, listen up!

Thou God of our idolatry, the press …
Thou fountain, at which drink the good and the wise …
Thou ever-bubbling spring of endless lies …
Like Eden's dread probationary tree …
Knowledge of good and evil is from thee.

Chapter 4:
The Wide-Open Mind

You may have known an "Annie"; in fact, you may have been an "Annie." You decide.

I met her through knowing her parents, and we became fast friends the instant we laid eyes on each other. She was as beautiful as I was plain and as wary as I was accepting. We seemed to need each other in order to balance out our lives for a season.

Her father often said that he wished that Annie was more like me, but I knew for a fact that he loved her just the way she was—a free spirit. Her mother competed with her for the affection of her father and sadly missed out on the relationship that the three of them could have had.

The real point to this story is that Annie had a wide-open mind. She was a seeker of the greatest magnitude, shining for a bit like a nova, and then crashing and burning, but always rising again like the phoenix espousing some new and exciting doctrine.

When we first met, she was deeply mystical and I was into teaching what I knew—the Bible. Somehow it took us only a year to make magical U-turns in our lives. She learned from me and I learned from her. But we never were on the same part of the path together at the same time.

Soon after that first year had passed, a shining idea snagged Annie's fancy, and she traveled to a place in her heart and mind that I could not follow, even though by that time I had also become a seeker of truth. We parted company at that time so that neither one of us would cloud the newfound clarity of the other.

It was a decade before we met again, and by that time I was part of the Christian ministry, through marriage. It all happened one day in the fall. Annie arrived at the door of the manse, unannounced. She was sporting cowboy boots, a Western-style hat, and the same élan that I had previously been drawn to. I invited her in.

Something about the look of her caught my attention as, with mind racing, Annie filled me in on all the major details of her life since we last were together. She had been married four times, had five children, and was living life just the way she had always wanted to—full of excitement and seeking the "new."

For the very first time I came to know a different, pitiable Annie. I do not know if it was from the vantage point that years of living my life had given me or that we had grown apart, but the words she said about the actions she had taken since our last meeting caused concern on my part. From the questions that I managed to wedge into the conversation, I found that there were no new books read, no new ideas formed, and not a word spoken about a belief system she had implemented. Annie seemed to be in exactly the same spiritual and emotional place she had been in as a young adult.

I had not necessarily needed to know what Annie had done with her life; I really wanted to know what she thought about what she had done with her life. What changes had she made to include others, and what amendments had she written for a belief system beyond self-gratification? Had she given thought to the devastation she had left churning in her wake?

Certainly by that time I had come to espouse the precept that a person must believe in something in order to live a grounded life. You must have knowledge of some ideas that work for you in your situation. And even though you seek new ideas that may make life richer and happier for you and your family, you need a base to build upon that is strong enough to support your own developing philosophy. There must be at least a set of rules that you discovered for yourself because, after all, the reason to seek is that you find at least some of the answers.

I agreed that Annie must search for the way she wanted to treat herself and the manner in which she wanted to interact with others; however, she must have paused at some point in her life to think and know that what she believed to be true was true for her. I thought of the children who Annie had and left behind to be raised by her former husbands. I thought about those husbands whom she unilaterally discarded in favor of new, more exciting, semi-permanent fixtures in her life.

What could I possibly have said to Annie that had not seemed like an uptight answer from a woman who had stopped her search in favor of a dull and quiet life? I felt that I had to be what she needed at this particular juncture in her life or she would not have arrived uninvited and seated herself across from me in my living room. Annie's wide-open mind had somehow signaled her to stop. It had led her to the only person she thought to have been brave enough to tell her what she needed to know and who would have survived the consequences. What a frightening responsibility that was, but I loved her enough to bear that for her.

Mission

Once I got Annie calmed down so that we were able to speak seriously and rationally to each other, I went to my writing desk and retrieved a pad and pencil from the middle drawer. She looked at me as if I had lost my mind when I extended them to her and told her to write. I didn't care what she wrote. I just wanted her to write. She hesitated for some time during which neither one of us said a word. And finally she began to write. As she wrote, her thoughts seemed to come to her faster and faster until she didn't have the time to write them down, and she became confused.

Annie raised her head from the pad with a look on her face that was very revealing. She had not only needed help, she wanted help. At that point I told her to tell herself to slow down and that her mind would do that for her. Now the old, quasi-cynical smile flashed across her face that meant "You're kidding, right?"

She trusted me enough, though, to carry through with her writing until I could tell that she was exhausted, and I asked her to let me see what she had written. Annie did not remember most of it, but I knew that this mental download must have been of help to her, for she had become the proverbial hamster on the wheel of life and had not known how to get off it.

Seated side by side, Annie and I searched for answers in what she had written. I knew that she was aware on a different level (her subconscious mind) what every answer was to every question she had ever asked the universe. These were some of the answers she discovered that day:

- The search was not the point. Finding useful answers was the point.
- She was addicted to the search.
- The needs of others who were dependent on her had to come before her own needs.
- She had mindlessly discarded those people in her life in favor of someone new and different.
- A mind with some of the answers is not a closed mind.
- Now that she consciously knew some of the answers, guilt should not be the remedy for the years they lay undiscovered.
- There were ways for those negative imprints to be healed, and she could use the mind tool of affirmation to do it.

Execution of the Process

Annie and I worked together to come up with a multitude of negative imprints and the corresponding positive affirmations to cover them. Some of them were so touching that in my moments alone I cried for her.

After weeks of searching and learning, we finally came to the final negative imprint. It was, of course, the underlying one of them all, her unforgiving attitude for the way that she was treated by her mother.

As a teenager, Annie had run away from home a few times only to be dragged back to the same emotional abuse that she had run from. When she became old enough she had split for good from her parents— and kept running. She apparently never stopped until she reached the front door of the manse years later and felt that she was finally safe.

It is almost as difficult to forgive parents for their shortcomings as it is to forgive yourself, and Annie needed that push that I could give her to resolve those years of negative imprints. But only an affirmation to cover all of the imprints surrounding her mother's treatment of her would be appropriate, and it was the only way that I knew of to effect the healing that Annie's life required.

It took a lot of thought and a lot of prayer to compose such an affirmation, and we spent time together doing that. We took the time to get to know each other again and to enjoy the company of our friendship, for we both knew that she had to return to the real life that she was now building, brick by brick, for herself. The most important affirmation that we composed together became this one: "Mother, I love you and I know that you love me."

Annie dropped all the accusations, the "she said/she said" words that in the end sounded petty and trite to her, and she forgave her mother. The hardest part of the whole thing was to let go of the story that had been the excuse for Annie to run wild and to give others the responsibility for how she ran her life.

By now you know the drill:

- Choose an appropriate affirmation of your own or use the one from Annie's story.

- Practice your affirmation until those negative imprints from your early life no longer carry negative emotion over into your conscious mind.
- Use the mirror technique.
- Be mindful of the words your subconscious mind tells you, and you decide whether they are true or not.
- Your life is precious—be good to yourself.

Annie came through all of the hard work like the champ I knew her to be. Instead of heaping hurt and blame on me for all she discovered about herself, she dug right in and began what was the most difficult transformation it had ever been my honor to witness.

By the time Annie passed from this life twenty years into her new and improved one, she had experienced once again the love of her children and the friendship of two of her former husbands. I thank God for the blessing that her life had become in her final days of suffering, for she had become a supreme example of the seeker using the answers she needed. Now it is time for you to do the same.

Classic Lines

Henrik Ibsen, the Norwegian playwright, wrote this self-evident answer to who you are: "What ought a man to be? Well, my short answer is himself" (*Peer Gant*, 1867).

I rather like this bit of writing by British writers W. C. Sellar and R. J. Yeatman in *1066 And All That* in the 1930s. "Gladstone ... spent his declining years trying to guess the answer to the Irish Question; unfortunately whenever he was getting warm, the Irish secretly changed the Question."

Chapter 5:
Get Out of the Boat

Rory and I had known each other for some years. Poor, shy, and fearfully silent would certainly describe her. Considering the fact that I was just about her opposite, we got along well.

We were distant members of the same family and would see each other perhaps twice a year if we were fortunate that year. My need to know her was because she was so very different from most of our outgoing and boisterous family.

Rory was an only child and, having few friends her age, found herself mostly in the company of adults. Even when we were twelve, she dressed like the adults in the family. She even spoke like them and used speech patterns that were sometimes antiquated. Both of her parents were college professors, and I had to ask Rory to explain some of the words that she used when we were together.

She was a talented artist who kept the secret even from her parents. I thought this to be a curious state of affairs but was thankful that she trusted me enough to dig into her hidden cache of paper sketches to bring them to light for me to "ooh" and "ah" over.

We learned to swim when we spent two weeks together one summer. She was a natural "water baby," while I had to be picked from the bottom of the creek so many times that my teeth were gritty when

I was done swimming, from all the mud I took in. It did not bother me too much, though, and I kept trying. For some reason Rory seemed frightened for me, or because of me, and rarely swam although she was great at it. She usually sat on the bank, wrapped in an old towel, and watched me splash around trying not to drown.

I always had friends, so I thought everyone did, until the birthday party. Rory was fourteen and her parents had invited all the girls in her class to the party. Besides myself there was only one girl who accepted the invitation. Her name was Grace, and even though she seemed to be Rory's clone, they did not get along very well. As for me, I got along pretty well with each of them since they did not want to play with each other, only with me. I felt so bad for Rory that I refused to play with the interloper unless Rory was included, and my dad was called to take me home before we even cut the cake.

When we were sixteen, I invited Rory to a prom. I had a friend who did not have a date for the dance and the two of them would be going double with my date and me. Since I had been attending dances and proms from the age of fourteen, I took it for granted she would want to go. And I was wrong. She protested so strongly that her mother grounded her for a week and she spent a good deal of time on the phone because she was bored, punishing me in the process.

Throughout our teenage years there was this back-and-forth action. I would try to get her to have fun, she would rebel and get punished, and through her, I would get punished.

You have to know this about me. I never give up, or hardly ever. But the last straw was when Rory refused to be in my wedding because she was shy. I gave her a choice of things to do. She could be a bridesmaid, a prompter standing beside the guest book, or she could stand inside the door to the sanctuary and pass out bulletins. I did not care. I just wanted her to be there for me.

Finally, during a rather testy phone call, I said something that I had heard the pastor say the Sunday before: "If you want to walk on water, you have to get out of the boat!"

Well, that made her cry, and she hung up on me. She did attend the wedding, however, wedged between her mother and father looking pinch-faced like it was the worst thing ever to be there at my wedding.

Yes, we finally gave up on each other. I allowed her to be who she was and no longer insisted that she change. She pushed me away—hard. I was sure that we were both happier for it. We have not seen each other in years, and we expect to only if we both get to heaven and we want to.

How could I have handled this situation so that Rory would finally feel good about herself and I would not feel like such a failure? I could not. I am sure that our youth had something to do with the way we both acted and reacted, but years have passed and I know that she holds nothing against me or I her. We would just rather not be in each other's company. Is this a valid way to live out our respective lives? Certainly if we both agree to it. My heart knows this, but my mind sometimes feels otherwise.

Mission

Guilt is an insidiously negative imprint, often sewn into the fabric of our subconscious with very complicated stitches. When I announced in this story that I almost never gave up, that statement was straight from my subconscious to my conscious mind and out my computer. And guilt was the negative imprint. Now you may think that is a stretch, but it is not, and this is why.

When we finally gave up on our so-called relationship, I felt guilty. Soon this convoluted, guilty imprint morphed into such things as: not being able to break a promise even when hospitalized to counsel a client, and jeopardizing my own life by trying to help someone who was totally out of control, on drugs, six feet two inches tall, and about 250 pounds. The excuse I gave myself at the time was that I wanted to protect the man's good name in the community, delivering a baby when the doctor was unable to arrive in time for a home birth—my only qualification being that I was the minister's wife who lived two doors down from the mommy. I could go on, but you understand that these were not instances of heroism on my part; they were instances of guilt.

I had difficulty solving serious life problems because my guilt-ridden subconscious had convinced me that no problem was too big for me to overcome. You noticed, of course, that it had not convinced me that there was no problem that I could not solve. So what I had done for much of my adult life was take my good old time learning that it was not tenacity that kept me from giving up; it was guilt. It was not a smart idea to dig in and not give up—ever. It was a stupid thing to do, so don't you ever do it!

Execution of the Process

The process of identifying the one real negative imprint that has bedeviled me most was complicated by the fact that tenacity for some reason was an ego booster. Not giving up made me feel somewhat pious sometimes. How strange is that?

Now it is your turn to ferret out those odd situations that you can identify as guilty negative imprints and to resolve them with positive affirmations. I will help you along the way, for guilt is a tricky imprint, often masquerading as a positive imprint as in the story above.

- Ascertain for yourself how guilt has complicated your life. Think of guilt in a new way. From as many sides of it as you can, examine your guilty imprints.
- Write a list of words or experiences that have placed you in a guilty state of mind.
- Compose one positive affirmation that will cover all the guilty imprints on your list. Mine is: "I overlay my guilt with sure knowledge."
- After each line on your list has been looked at closely and overlaid with the positive affirmation you have composed, blot each line out with a black felt-tip pen.
- When your list is completed and you are sure that the

affirmation that you chose has overlaid each instance of a guilty imprint, rejoice in your newfound freedom.

Step out into the sunshine and be happy. You are not helpless anymore because you have done the work with your own affirmations to overlay your own negative imprints, and you are in control of the guilty imprints. You will still be reminded of them, but trust that your repeated affirmations will prevail. I have done it myself, and I am confident that you will be able to complete this work in yourself so that your future will be more happily stable and comfortable for you to live in.

Classic Lines

This very short clip will mean something different to each of you. Give it a try. See if you can fit it to one of your guilty negative imprints. It was written by Lloyd Osborne in 1889 in *The Wrong Box*. "What hangs people … is the unfortunate circumstance of guilt."

Chapter 6:
Harry and His Walk to the Present

Harry took his place in the cozy chair that I had prepared for him in my study. A soft, often-washed blue blanket lined it. The lights were dimmed and the shades were pulled down almost to the windowsill. A small lamp created all the ambient light required for the session.

It was not often that a man screwed up his courage to speak to a Christian counselor, especially one whom he knew personally. But here he was and there I was sitting directly opposite him in another chair, swathed exactly like the one he was sitting in.

I tried not to have preconceived ideas about the way this particular session would go, and I moved gently forward in this case. But at first it seemed that I did not have to do that, since he came to me in a lighthearted mood. He talked animatedly about the last time we had been together. His mood nevertheless sent up so many red flags that I wondered about the wisdom of continuing the counseling session.

I had tried my best to direct him to a pastor in our area, but after two meetings with the man, he came complaining to the manse one day, insistent that I help him since a friend had again turned him back in my direction. He had checked back with that friend, who thought it would be best for me to counsel Harry.

That did not cut much ice with me, since I did not know this friend or care much about what he thought I should do. But a pleading call from Harry's wife, Charlotte, caused me to rethink my rigid rule of not counseling people whom I knew personally.

I ticked off the reasons on one hand why I should not take this man on. When I came to the very last reason, I wished that circumstances were different. The simple fact that Harry was not a member of any of the churches that I counseled for meant that I was not bound by the judgments of their councils. But still I was wary about taking on his problem just for the reason that if the sessions went south on me, I had no one's decision to fall back on but my own.

So there we sat. Harry joked while I tried desperately to get the session on track. Finally he got up from his chair. That was a sign to me that he was actually changing his mood, and it was not necessarily a good one. Something in the back of my mind put me on alert, and it was a good thing, for he soon turned angrily in my direction, spit out some foul words about what he thought of me, and slammed the door of the study. A few seconds later, I heard the front door slam so hard it shook the manse, and I heard his car roar away from the curb in front of my neighbor's house. Did I follow him, most assuredly not? He was actually a danger to me and to himself.

Thankfully a call to George, our local police chief who could check up on him, confirmed that Harry had arrived home safely and was talking with his neighbor when George drove up to ostensibly say "Hi."

Since the chief was a friend to both Harry and his neighbor, he had joined their conversation and George's return call deemed Harry to be just fine. Of course, because I knew that he was decidedly not fine, I called Charlotte to put her on alert. I need not have bothered because, according to her, she was always on alert when Harry was around and had put measures in place to make sure that she was relatively safe. When I heard this, I realized that this case was more than I could handle.

I tried to tie up all the loose ends that dangled from the counseling session I had just had with Harry so that I could pass them to someone more adept at helping him with his problems. In the short term, the one loose end that I really struggled with was the safety of Harry himself.

Very early the next morning, I got a frantic call from Charlotte. It seemed that Harry got out of bed during the night to go to the bathroom and never came back. Charlotte had gone back to sleep and just gotten up to an empty house, and worse yet, her car was gone.

I called George with the news, and he hit the road to try to find Harry—and he soon did. He reported back to me that Charlotte's car was sitting in a ditch apparently empty, but when George investigated the car more closely, he found that Harry had somehow rolled onto the floor in front of the seats. He was breathing loudly, and George thought he may have drunk himself into a stupor, until he saw the empty pill bottle that had rolled between the seats.

George immediately called the number for the ambulance that was parked in the middle of town awaiting an emergency. Ours was a small town, and no one needed to sound a siren for what was considered a personal problem. The ambulance crept unobtrusively out of town with Harry inside it. It was a plus to living in this valley that everyone knew you and protected you from your own stupidity if they could—including law enforcement.

By the time the ambulance arrived at the hospital twenty miles away, Harry had awakened and asked the driver's wife, who was his attendant on the twenty-mile trip, where he was. She sat stone-faced and pretended not to hear his question, which he repeated several times. Harry was soon put on a litter to take him from the ambulance to the ER where he was to be evaluated. After I hung up from George's call, I phoned Charlotte. And giving her as few facts about Harry as I could for her to worry about, I said that I would be at her front door in ten minutes to follow her to the hospital.

I sat in the waiting room while Charlotte paced for the better part of two hours until she was called to the desk and told to bring her car around to the drive-through in front of the door to the ER. Harry was pronounced okay to go home and sleep off the rest of what he had ingested. The attending had made the decision not to pump his stomach but to let him ride the whole thing out, which turned out not to be the brightest decision he had made that day. I hugged Charlotte as she gave me her good news, walked to the parking lot to retrieve my car, and left for home.

I heard later that it was quite a wild ride for Charlotte, up and then down the mountain and into the valley as Harry kept trying to take the wheel from her. They arrived at their home in about twenty-five minutes, which was pretty good on those winding mountain roads.

Immediately upon arriving home, Charlotte was dispatched to the manse by Harry to beg me to take him back as a client. He had told his wife that he was almost sure he had hurt my feelings with his outburst the day before. That should have been the least of Harry's worries as far as I was concerned, but it did give me a chance to speak with Charlotte. I spoke at length to her about Harry's need to see a real physician, and I begged her to support me in this decision. But for some reason she thought that since he seemed to be able to calm himself after each episode, he just needed someone to talk to, and he had chosen me.

Sometimes when women act in such a pitiable way, it brings tears to my eyes and a lump to my throat so hard that I think I will surely choke. I understood—I really did—how Charlotte felt because I have been there. In my case I had, for a while, closed my eyes in denial that a relative really needed help and that if I loved her enough, her life would return to normal. I was, however, aware that it was not a true thought and rarely, if ever, played out that way.

Within weeks it became rudely apparent that Harry acted out only to females, for he had seriously injured Charlotte. Unfortunately, the two of them had hit their own personal bottom before they finally realized that Harry indeed had a serious problem that the three of us were unable to fix.

Harry had to be hospitalized and medicated for some time until he and his male therapist got a handle on what Harry's problem was. It was not soon enough to save their marriage, however, and the short of it was that they divorced and each of them in turn moved away, remarried, and went on with their lives.

I felt that it must have been God's will that they never had children, for I was quite sure that it would have been devastating to them in the end, carrying forward the negative imprint of hatred toward the opposite sex, which they could have absorbed innocently from a broken father and a mother who made excuses for him.

Everyone mentioned in this story has passed, even George, so I feel that telling their stories now would neither hurt them nor anyone else and that their example may be of help to others.

Mission

After his doctor released him, Harry insisted that he meet with me to fill me in on all facets of his problem. He was molested by a woman when he was a boy, and he experienced flashbacks that so angered him that he became violent and unable to control his words or actions. These flashbacks appeared unbidden, he once thought. But through intense counseling, the trigger was eventually identified. It was the presence of a strong woman who he felt expected more of him than he was willing to give (the counseling session). He could not recall what the words were that I said in our session that triggered him, but he knew that I thought he was being an ass and that I wanted him to settle down and get on with what he perceived his problem to be.

I explained to Harry that his negative imprint was still there. But the two of us were able to work together (a miracle in itself) and found a way around that imprint by practicing appropriate affirmations. Harry proceeded remarkably well with only a few days of instruction from me. I was surprised that he felt it meaningful to return to my counseling chair considering that even recounting his problem to me could have been an additional trigger for his imprint. I explained all of that up front but he was certainly ready to change his mind, which is very important to this process.

When Harry felt sure that he had the upper hand in his battle with that negative imprint, he moved to upstate New York, where I heard he had married a woman much younger than himself.

After a period of time, Charlotte came back to have lunch, and we chatted about the small town that she had moved to, near the border of Maryland and Pennsylvania. She was dating the pastor of the new church that she attended, and the relationship had become serious. However, she held back from marrying him for some time.

When asked, I assured her that my work had been tough but the joy of the pastorate life was more than enough to make it worthwhile, and I wished her well. I received short notes from her occasionally during the next few years, which I kept as treasures, only because she sounded so very happy.

Execution of the Process

I had not been part of Harry's healing; I only knew the result of it. I would not presume to tell you how his healing took place. If his case was brought forward to me today, this is what I would do. It is some of the same advice I gave Harry and Charlotte many years ago:

- Tell the story you need to tell.
- If the counselor recommends that you be released to a physician, take the recommendation seriously.
- If you do not take the advice seriously, you should accept that there will be a warning to those close to you that the situation is very precarious and that you have been released from the counselor to a physician.
- There must be counseling support available for you and your family in order to handle any fallout from the change of mind you experience from the advice of a physician.
- A closing session with a counselor is in order to instruct you as a couple in the method to overlay your negative imprints with new and positive affirmations.

Although their lives together had not returned to normal—or the way it once was, as Charlotte had hoped—I believe God blessed these two people as they lived their separate, very meaningful lives.

Classic Lines

"All the business of war, and indeed all the business of life, is to endeavour to find out what you don't know by what you do" (attributed to Wellington in *The Croker Papers*, 1885).

"For fools rush in where angels fear to tread" (copied from *An Essay on Criticism* by Alexander Pope in 1711).

Chapter 7:
The Obedience of Job and Overcoming Self-Pity

I know. You were expecting the patience of Job, weren't you? Well, obedience was what saved Job's life, and I will prove it to you in this small chapter.

For those who have not read the book of Job from the Bible, in short here is how the story goes:

The tale of Job began by telling the reader that not everyone on that day in history was full of nonsense and wickedness. There was at least one man who displayed a splendid spirit, and his name was Job. Job was a rich man, which proves that being rich does not necessarily mean that you have no soul to speak of, for Job had a great family, and they were (every one of them) blessed with all the comforts of their world.

"It is easy to be happy if you are rich," we say, but what if you suddenly become poor? Would you be miserable like other poor people, or would you still manage to be happy and to praise God? Where would your faith be if suddenly everything and almost everyone was taken away from you, and the wife who was left to you cursed you and told you to go ahead and die?

It sounds radical but that is essentially what happened to Job. God decided to prove to Satan that Job would still keep the faith, even if he lost everything and everyone dear to him. And God set about testing Job, for He was sure that he would remain steadfast in his love toward God and give Him praise no matter what happened to change Job's life.

In the first instance of God's testing, a storm came to the desert where Job and his family resided. Job's house was destroyed by that storm, and all of his children, who were assembled inside it, were crushed to death. Most of us would have cried uncle at that point, but wait—there is more. Another storm came up and killed all of Job's sheep. Then robbers came and stole his camels, oxen, and asses.

And as a final test, God tried Job's body. He gave him leprosy, at which time everyone fled from him because it was such a dreaded and contagious disease. So now Job was alone, childless, and cursed by a fatal disease. But all that he uttered concerning his situation was this: "The Lord gave, and the Lord has taken away; blessed be the name of the Lord."

One day while Job waited, perhaps a little concerned about what would happen to him next, some of his friends came to visit him. I can imagine that they stood far off—the leprosy, you know. And just as some friends do, they brought words of comfort to him—by saying that Job himself was the cause of his own calamity and that he must have sinned big-time somewhere down the line for all of this to have happened to him.

That was the final straw—too much for Job, and he lost it. He rebelled against all that had happened to him and cursed the day that he was born.

When everyone had settled down and his friends had departed, Job thought better of what he had voiced and tried to think of something to say that would mean that he was sorry without really saying the words—some really nice things, such as "You are so wise, oh God, and great—the one and only God of the Jews."

Job realized that he had more than stepped over the line, but the

"S" word just would not come out of his mouth, and God was not buying anything he had to say at that point.

This is when God and Job had a heart-to-heart talk. In general, God gave Job a talking to, and wanted to know from him just when he had become so smart and felt that he knew everything. Because, in God's eyes—He was the one here in the beginning—He was the only all-knowing One.

Then Job started to feel sorry for himself and groveled like we sometimes do, saying, "Oh right, everything is all my fault, I think that I will just go out there in that dung heap and die."

Does that sound familiar at all to you? But God showed his mastery of tough love and told Job to get up out of there and straighten himself up.

Job finally broke down and confessed to God, saying "I am vile. I do not even know what to say to you, God," and he put his hand across his mouth.

And because Job humbled himself and, in an acceptable way to God, apologized and showed his obedience, God blessed him again and gave him more family, more herds, and more of everything than He had taken away from Job. And this inspired Job to live the rest of his life praising God.

Mission

What can we learn from Job's story? Surely it was not that he was patient, because when he was given more burdens than he thought he could take, he cursed the day that he was born, among other things that God did not take too kindly to.

I think that even God realized that He had taken things a little too far in the testing department, but when He tried to explain to Job why He took issue with what Job had said, Job played the part of the poor baby and really got told off. Not until Job repented and showed obedience to God did he get returned to him the blessings that filled his life with joy.

In every one of the books I have written, at some point I try to make the case for knowing what you know. Do not stand in midair, blowing one way in the wind and then the other, trying to live your life effectively. I urge you to get down to the basics of what you believe, and then you will not fly apart at every illness or problem that you have. Now all of Job's issues were severe and any one of them may have taken you down, but in the end Job knew where to turn, what to do, and what to say in order to be blessed.

I will not presume to talk you through an altar call or any other religious rite, but I do want you to think about a belief system that works for you. There used to be a saying—but it is not as prevalent as it used to be—and it goes like this: "There are no atheists in foxholes."

When everything is coming down around you and you think that you are going to die, you will call upon your God, that source that gives you comfort and strength to go through what you certainly must in this life.

Execution of the Process

The story of Job shows us that when he was tested by God, he finally broke. At first he kept his faith in God and praised Him even though he was very sick and had lost everything and everyone who was dear to him. All that it took to change Job's mind were the words of some friends who had dropped by to chat with him. And that chat stirred up a negative imprint harbored in Job's mind so that he cursed God and himself. What a turnaround for him to make. All it took was a trigger to activate loathing and self-pity in Job that might have cost him his very life. Job actually began to believe that he was to blame for all that had happened to him. Of course, when you listen to what others say instead of staying your ground and working through your problems, you are displaying to one and all that you have no control over the negative imprints harbored in your subconscious mind.

Now you might think that this scenario does not describe something that you would be tempted to do—curse yourself and God—not you,

you say. If you were Job, after everything and everyone were taken away and you were assured by those who knew you well that everything that happened to you was your own fault, what would you do? Was it possible that what Job's friends came to tell him triggered the negative imprint of self-pity? Could someone in his life have said to him, "It is all your fault?"

Has anyone ever said to you, "It is all your fault?"

Take for granted then that you have this negative imprint of self-pity and that it has been triggered, perhaps a few times or many times.

- The first thing I want you to do is to compose an affirmation. This affirmation is to be very specific in order to cover a very specific negative imprint: self-pity.

- Take that positive affirmation and speak it into those eyes in the mirror. You may tear up a bit, but if you persevere, gently but adamantly, you will talk yourself out of self-pity mode and into a more mature frame of mind.

It is never really easy to practice your affirmations, but they are so worthwhile to your well-being. Please do not get weary or bored with them.

Classic Lines

This is a short piece by Italian poet Dante and is contained in *La Divina Commedia*. It rings true to the imprint of self-pity: "O pure and noble conscience, how bitter a sting to thee is a little fault!" He wrote it between 1308 and 1321.

Chapter 8:
In Stormy Seas

Entitlement—you hear the word often in these days of bailouts and fraudulent schemes of all types, and you wonder if this concept is innate in each of us. Do you tend to try to get away with what you think you can? And have you, in our own unique way, made a space for entitlement in your heart and mind? I would say the answer to that is probably yes. Now let me explain what I mean by that last statement because I can hear you grumbling now about my lack of understanding.

Somehow it is always the other guy who is in the wrong—who expects too much of his God and his fellowman. Go with me into your own heart and mind and dig around a little. Ask yourself these questions. Do you always say "Thank you"?

One of the basic tenets you learn just as soon as you can form words is the meaning of "thank you." Not only that, you learn when to say it. Please do not excuse yourself by saying that you were not brought up that way. If you are over the age of five, you most certainly have heard and understood the concept of "thank you," and you began to include it in your own speech patterns as soon as you were cued by the situation at hand to do so.

When you hosted a party, did you push to the head of the buffet line? After all, it was you who had forked over the money for the food.

Have you chosen the most comfortable chair in the room even though there is someone older in attendance who you knew to be more in need of it? I experienced not only one but two people (father and daughter) who were in a room full of close family members, one of whom was in her nineties and quite frail. Each of them took aim for the cushiest chair in the room that had been reserved for the ninety-year-old, somehow getting in front of her and trying to sit in the same chair from different sides of it. Okay, I admit it—that stunt was too much even for me, and I stepped in, almost graciously, to give the seat to the person for whom it was intended.

When have you done something kind for someone else without first thinking of yourself and how that simple act may benefit you? Have you insisted on having the best for yourself, such as tailor-made clothes, while your family shopped for clothing at the thrift store? After all, you bring in the money for the family. You are entitled to get what you want and get it first.

When you became ill, did you expect your loved ones to gather around and wait on you after you have vetted the thought that if your loved ones ever became ill, they should not expect you to care for them?

If you were put in charge of something, have you always abused the power extended to you in good faith, knowing that you can?

It may feel good to you if you can say to yourself that you have not bilked your friends out of millions of dollars and you have never committed insurance fraud. But the little things in life that you thoughtlessly do add up to who you are, and sometimes add all the way up to the power grab that some of you have executed. In other words, when you got away with what you would term the "little things," you tended to escalate to bigger and bigger possibilities, and when you felt more powerful, you also felt entitled to do more of what you wanted to do, no matter who it impacted. After all, you were elected to political office and no matter if it was as chief dogcatcher, that power invested in you should have given you the latitude to do those things that were illegal and/or unethical for anyone else to have done.

Let's pretend that you were very rich. When you went shopping with your entourage, you generally carried with you no means to pay for what you chose to buy for yourself. You just pointed to the person next to you, said "Take care of that," and continued on your way.

You took advantage of others, and no matter how big or how small that advantage was, it was unacceptable in almost any culture. Many television show plots gravitated to this very thing. Some programs even glorified unfair competition or uneven competition. I am sure that when you continually fed on that fare, you at some point deemed it acceptable to have perpetrated a fraud on an unwary person.

Because your "idol" involved himself in dogfights or maybe you were invited to a bullfight while visiting with friends in another country, you somehow thought it was okay to have participated in it all and gave yourself a pass to have done it. You have assuaged your guilty feelings with the thought that some of these things were culture-based and colorful. You were fooling yourself. I know, I get all wound up about this subject—and I wish more people would do the same.

Mission

Would it be possible to somehow, someway, get to the point that is represented by Namaste, to recognize in another that same source that is in yourself so that you are able to treat another as you do yourself?

There are so many ways for you to get caught up in the net of entitlement and arrogance. After all, everyone is doing it. Our government even promotes it at every level—so what should you do? You really have to make up your own mind about these things, but maybe you will gain some insight into your situation by learning from others—just maybe.

There are ways that you can help yourself, even when you lose your job, for instance. You do not have to rely on the government to assist you. Here are some things that I have learned about that subject: Do not be so proud that you insist on a new job at the same level as that of your previous one, and if one job does not do it for you and your family, get two jobs or even three. Do not excuse yourself from doing this because you fear that it may be too difficult—you will be surprised at what you can do, and that will give you confidence to do an even better job.

Do not let anyone tell you that all that good work, sometimes done in the discharge of menial jobs, is for nothing and does not look good on your résumé. Employers are always looking for the confidence borne of the hard worker, the creative earner, and the stick-to-it attitude that demonstrates that you are self-reliant.

Always be on the lookout for another job in your field or a good job earning more money. Do this just so you can say good-bye to one of your jobs. What a good feeling it is when you no longer need to work such long hours and you are able to bid your third job farewell, and then your second one. And finally you are left with one good job, with upward mobility and a good salary working only five days a week. Then you can pat yourself on the back and tell yourself you have done well.

Execution of the Process

Examine the subjects of the previous thoughts. They are pride, fear, making excuses, and listening to others who may or may not have your best interests at heart. Instead of listening to the negative thought that fast-forwards through you mind, this time first go with your gut. Who and what do you want to show to the world in what may have, at first, amounted to a disaster in your life? Make up your own mind what that should be.

- Now it is your job to search for that negative imprint that prevents you from being that special person you envision and compose a positive affirmation to cover it.
- Your negative imprint could be fear that you would let down those who depended on you. If you are the eldest child in the family, this imprint could be triggered a lot.

- By now you are adept at covering negative imprints stored in your subconscious mind for years, and now it is time to do something about this one.

- Do what works for you now. Perhaps you have chosen an affirmation that singularly addresses fear. A phrase, such as the one included in the **Classic Lines,** is placed at the end of this chapter. It is a famous quote and must have been used by tens of thousands of people just to remove themselves from the horrors of war. I have taken the liberty of paraphrasing: "I have nothing to fear but fear it self."

My hope is that you were able to gain something from these examples and you will learn to "sail on stormy seas" and arrive on the shore safely. You may feel the need to wear your life jacket, but you can do it. I trust you. Surely you can trust yourself.

Classic Lines

This line was spoken by Franklin Delano Roosevelt during his inaugural address on March 4, 1933: "The only thing we have to fear is fear itself." The president was serializing the events that were happening in the world at that time and this idea to America and to the rest of the world which was in turmoil at the time.

Chapter 9:
Dancing with Mario

I am going to insert a story here that is a little different from the previous ones in that another person unwittingly took charge of a friend's negative imprint and instructed her in the affirmation that he gently covered it with. His name was Mario. Hers was Karen.

She was a newly divorced mom who had not expected to be in that situation. Most women hardly know what hits them when it happens, and she was no different. But through all the mess of attorneys, leaving one home for the next one, and finding a new job and appropriate schools for her three young girls, she found that this serious upset to her family was hardly manageable for her on so many levels.

But Karen was determined not to let her children down and to try to smooth this very traumatic transition and make it work for them instead of against them. The chance for upward mobility in her new job was something that Karen had only dreamed of. But the pay was not enough to take care of her children, let alone herself, and she took on two part-time jobs to make up for the delta between what she earned and what they required.

Time to grieve the loss of marriage, home, and security for her children was nonexistent, and that was probably for the best, because she considered time with her one teen and two tweens her most important job.

Enter Mario. Mario came into Karen's new life at the busiest time. She did not have much time for new acquaintances and, besides, she was still feeling raw from the ordeal she and her children had gone through that past year. She also had trust issues up to her eyebrows because of it.

So it was probably an inopportune time for Mario to drive up to the curb as Karen was walking up the street to her home from one of her jobs. Out of the corner of her eye, she noticed the little red sports car sidle up beside her as she tried to walk faster and faster. Then a young man lowered the window of his car and called something to her that she could not quite make out, so she stopped walking, thinking that he was asking for directions. As it turned out he had wanted to introduce himself, just trying to be neighborly.

Up went the wall that she had sturdily built around herself in the time since the divorce. Karen was sure he noticed, but Mario kept on talking, continuing to engage her in a conversation that she wanted no part of. And when it ended a few moments later, she remembered nothing that he had said, but her eyes followed the little red car as he drove away until it passed from her field of vision.

It was a few weeks later that she found Mario waiting at the entrance to her development. He looked so unassuming and totally harmless he stood in the sunshine, leaning against the passenger door of his car. He was possibly three inches taller than she was and smiled widely as she approached.

Karen nodded as she tried to walk by him, but he was having none of it and began walking beside her. She was completely taken back as they approached her home. She thought of walking past it so that Mario would not know exactly where she lived, but he walked slightly ahead of her and turned in the walkway leading to her front door.

Stalker, she thought angrily, but he stopped and let her lead the way to her tiny porch.

Mario propped himself against the wrought iron of the porch

railing and gave her that wide grin of his. Karen was so flustered that she did the same, thinking that if he waited on her porch all night she was not going to invite him in. But she quickly came to her senses and told him that she had to go in and make supper for the girls. He stood up straight and looked her in the eye only to say that he would like to take her dancing some Saturday evening if she would honor him with her company. And then, without waiting for an answer, he walked off down the street toward his parked car.

More than a month later, Karen received a telephone call at work from Mario. He must have had access to a base directory because she had certainly not given her number to him, and she was coolly polite as he asked her once again if she would go dancing with him—the following Saturday night.

Suddenly there was so much dead air between them that Mario clicked the phone wondering if she was still on the line. And of course she was. She just did not have a clue how to answer him, and then for some reason she blurted out "Yes!"

She could "hear" him grinning as he spoke some kind words to her, told her he would be picking her up at her home at nine o'clock, and hung up.

Karen phoned him the next morning—retrieving his number from a card that he had given her on the first encounter they had by the side of Lincoln road—to tell him that she had changed her mind and would not be going dancing with him on Saturday evening.

Mario was quiet on the other end of the line for what seemed to her to be a very long time but was probably only a few seconds. Just as she was about to replace the receiver in its cradle, he sighed and said, "But you promised that you would go dancing with me."

He spoke quietly and with a voice full of patience. It would have been so much easier, Karen thought, if he would have gotten angry or hung up the phone. She could have felt somehow justified in turning him away. But he did not do either one and she could not break her promise because of it.

Saturday night came more quickly than she wanted it to. Karen slipped into a little aqua dress with a flirty hem and put on her dancing shoes. It had been such a long time since she had worn them. They looked a little shabby, *but who would notice?* she asked herself.

Mario arrived at her front door precisely at nine o'clock. She had pumped herself up for a full hour before by dancing around the living room, and inadvertently being the comic relief for two of her girls as she had done so.

Karen took Mario's arm and paraded through the front doors to the tune of her giggling daughters. He gently helped her step down into the low-slung vehicle, returned to his side of it, and, being careful not to lean too closely toward her, they drove off.

They soon arrived at the club where they were to have dinner and dance, parked the car, and followed a few other couples up to the large double doors at the front of the club. And there stood a gentleman who was checking membership cards. He waved them in, and she could hear elevator music in the background as they entered a very large room with a dance floor as big as Utah.

Around the perimeter of that floor were tables covered in lavender linens, each with a small vase of flowers in the center of it. One of those tables had been reserved for Mario and guest, and the maître d' graciously took Karen's elbow and walked her to it as Mario followed behind.

Mario's manners were impeccable as he seated her so that she had an unobstructed view of the stage full of instruments and amps. As Karen covertly surveyed the rest of the tables, her mind was put at ease—thankfully, she knew no one. Meanwhile, Mario ordered drinks, and a waiter brought hors d'oeuvres to the table just as the lights were lowered and a spot was trained on the now-assembled band. All through a very lovely dinner they played soft jazz, so Karen had not felt the need to speak until spoken to.

After the tables were cleared, the band music took an upbeat turn as they kicked off the first set with a cha-cha. It was one step that Karen had never danced. Mario, ignoring her whispered protests, got up from his chair, gently pulled her up from hers, and, not wanting to make a scene, Karen walked with him to the center of the dance floor.

Mario smiled his broadest smile at her as he drew her close and whispered the steps in her ear. Backward she danced to the count of one, two, cha cha cha. Forward she stepped one, two, cha, cha, cha. Mario turned her, swung her, and stepped back and forward with her until Karen was a little out of breath. As the music's spicy beat ramped down to an ending, Mario swung her around twice, and with her head swimming, Karen wondered how he had so deftly and easily controlled her body as they danced. She had felt so ungainly for the first couple of seconds, but all that disappeared with the whispered instruction she was given for the cha-cha.

With the dance at its end, Karen stood away from Mario and looked around the dance floor. She had been oblivious to the fact that they were the only ones on it and that everyone else had gathered in clusters around the perimeter of it. Then they applauded. Mario took her hand and pulled her down into a mock bow as the band began playing once more. She tried to escape to their table, but listening to the waltz they were playing, she gave in and they headed for the middle of the room.

Again Mario was in control as they glided around the huge circle that was the dance floor, bisected it, and danced around the room once more whirling and turning, making Karen glad that she had worn the frothy little dress she had on. When the waltz came to its elegant end, they floated back to their table.

Mario seated her and walked around to his side of the table. Leaning over slightly toward her, he softly told Karen how great she was on the dance floor and that couple up every Saturday night. Not returning his intense gaze, she looked at the tablecloth in front of her and mumbled that she would think about it.

They chatted through the next number, but when the band started playing the fourth piece, she had not recognized it but thought it was probably a slow dance. As they returned to the floor and before she realized that they were listening to the verse of a very fast jitterbug,

Mario already had her tightly in his arms. But she felt safe there and trusted him that she could dance to any piece she really wanted to dance to, and Karen relaxed.

Mission

Mario confessed to her on the short ride back to her home that he had requested those special numbers that the band played that evening. And the band had played a wide variety of dance music that had added up to a tutorial of rhythm that he thought Karen would enjoy. He had not needed to confess to her because she had figured out early on that this was a planned evening for Mario and his new dance partner. In his defense, he wanted to teach her that she could do anything she really wanted to—even smile, which she had surely done that evening.

Karen and Mario formed a couple on the dance floor for two more years and went dancing at his club every Saturday night that they were able to. Karen gained back her confidence and, more important to Mario, learned to smile again.

Mario managed to fox-trot, jitterbug, and waltz Karen out of her sadness and taught her the confidence that she thought she had lost and the trust that she felt would never be replaced.

Execution of the Process

Mario, beyond a shadow of a doubt, had used the mind tool of affirmation to its fullest extent—unknowingly. And here is the way you can tell:

- Mario treated Karen with kindness so that the negative imprint of cruelty was rendered impotent.
- He was patient with her and encouraged her when the negative imprint of worthlessness raised its ugly head.
- Mario taught her that he could be trusted so that he could overlay the negative imprint of her very valid trust issues.

So, what could you say that Mario's chosen affirmation was for the overlay of the negative imprints that Karen displayed? Perhaps it would sound something like this: "You are loved. You are valued. You can trust me." And he said these words to Karen for two years until she believed them to be true.

Perhaps there is someone who needs you—someone you work with, attend church with, or go to the gym with. Reach out in patience, kindness, and friendship. You never know when you may need a "Mario."

Classic Lines

To get back to the subject of the dance, I will leave you to ponder these words written by the Irish poet William Butler Yeats: "O body swayed to music/O brightening glance/How can we know the dancer from the dance?" He wrote them in 1928 in *Among School Children.*

Chapter 10:
Helen and Her Second Marriage

Helen had been unmarried for twenty-five years. Those years held pain and pleasure, negatives and positives, as they do for most people. But when she made the choice to remarry all hell broke loose, and I mean that literally.

After a month of marriage, Helen asked for an annulment. James refused, and she ranted! There were people she wanted to blame, and on the very top of that list had been the man who still called himself her husband. She was convinced that she had been duped into marriage.

Helen became ill. Her still-lithe body and her usually compliant spirit rebelled, and it made life miserable for James and herself. Her dismal attitude spilled over into other parts of her life as she conjured up the sordid story of her disappointment in her marriage. And she told it to anyone who would listen. After a year and a half, she finally pulled up roots and left him.

It took only a short time after that for Helen to convince her body that James was really out of her life and two months to clear her head well enough to think rationally. She soon settled into a great little apartment without television, radio, or newspaper, and enjoyed the quiet sanctuary she had created for herself. And as she took up writing poetry again, as she had always done during the sad times in her life, she found that she had almost enough of it to bind into a slender book that summed up her errors and broken dreams. But she knew that would never happen as she read through them, finding them way too personal.

Meanwhile, James contacted his attorney, as Helen had already done, and the sides were chosen for the mini-war that she decided not to engage in.

They had tried marriage counseling before she separated from James, but he had decided for some reason to stonewall Dr. Jeff, and the hard work that Helen had done fell to the ground like so many dead leaves while James had sat silent through appointment after appointment. One day, halfway through their session, Dr. Jeff finally told Helen to leave the SOB and that she would be just fine, and Helen stalked out of the room. It took another year before she took his advice.

Time passed slowly in her cozy space, but the strangest part of all was that this grand mistress of multitasking was not bored. And when Angie, a friend of hers, asked her to attend a soccer game, Helen was reluctant to go. But after some coaxing, she reluctantly agreed. It would do her good, she had thought. The poetry was piling up fast, a testament to her mood.

When the day of the game arrived, Helen really wanted to cancel, but she reconsidered, walking the ten minutes or so to the soccer field to meet Angie. Partway through a very exciting and very loud game, her peripheral vision caught a glimpse of a man walking toward her on the bleachers, but she was caught up in the game, that is until she felt something touch the back of her hair. She automatically leaned forward so the person could pass behind her.

The next thing that happened startled her, and Helen almost screamed as the man she had seen walking the bleachers leaned over her, touching her hair and saying in a low creepy voice, "Would you like to share your blanket with me?"

She turned and glared at him in response as she pulled her borrowed blanket close around her so that he could not possibly have done so. He looked startled in return and, drawing himself up to his full height, walked dejectedly down the bleachers. Her eyes followed him until he walked down the steps and out the left gate of the field. She suddenly had a sinking feeling and, turning toward Angie, she started to say, "What was all that," and then she caught a glimpse of her angry face.

"Don't you know who that was?" Angie asked, her voice rising way beyond high C on the scale.

Helen thought that should have been fairly evident as she prepared herself for another salvo from Angie, who continued sputtering like a match in the wind.

It seemed that Helen had, by her attitude, driven off the "catch of the day." He was a celebrated coach—that very field whose bleachers they sat on was named after him. The town revered him to the point that the street that ran the length of town was named for him. Angie went on and on until Helen rudely stopped her. "Okay, I got it. His name is Hertzler!"

Angie was not finished, however, and soon let it slip that she had pulled a few strings to get him to the point where he wanted to meet Helen. It seemed that she had cooked up this whole mess to surprise her, making her wonder if Angie had known her at all.

Then it was Helen's turn to be ticked, and she turned on Angie with a sour speech of her own, berating her for not even telling poor Mr. Hertzler that it was a surprise. Helen told her in no uncertain terms that she was in no frame of mind to date another man who had just lost his wife, run out of clean underwear, and was searching for a woman to do the wash.

She hissed all of this in Angie's direction, threw the borrowed blanket in her lap, and took the bleachers two at a time until she gained the field and headed out the south gate for home.

As her little home came into sight, Helen's eyes filled with tears, and as she started up the front steps to her apartment, they spilled down her cheeks. Thankfully she had not locked the front door because a neighbor was hurrying toward her to say "Hi."

Helen waved, hurried into her living room, and closed the door. She could not believe how bitter and cruel she had become. She thought she was doing just fine living in the comfortable nest that she had made for herself—getting divorced.

Helen hunted down her wedding ring and, finding it in the chest of drawers underneath some sweaters she had stored there for the summer, jerked it unto the third finger of her left hand. Then at three o'clock on that sunny afternoon, she crawled into bed fully clothed, pulled the covers over her head, and fell asleep.

Just when Helen thought she was "handling" things, Angie threw her the wrong end of a boomerang. And it had made her feel that it was past time for her to take a hard look at the new life she had so effortlessly carved out for herself. She had even deemed it necessary to replace her wedding ring on her finger to warn off anyone who may be interested in her. Helen had discovered that day at the soccer game that something was terribly wrong with her plans for the future and her ability to proceed with them.

The anger that she felt when meeting Mr. Hertzler appalled her, and her face burned just thinking about how she had treated a perfect stranger so callously. He had obviously meant her no harm, but she was so quick to judge him.

As for Angie's "man of her dreams," he had made an honest mistake by saying what he said, but what was Helen's excuse for the way she acted? It was too easy to make it all Angie's fault, and Helen vowed to make it up to her as she searched her heart and mind for the reason she had changed so much in her few short months living alone.

In the next couple of days, Helen's search turned over some very heavy rocks as she spent hours meditating in the only space where she felt safe and peaceful: the bedroom of her apartment. And what she came up with was a sad set of circumstances. Angie had inadvertently triggered a negative imprint that Helen was not aware of.

Mission

The negative setup in Helen's subconscious was this: Her soon-to-be ex-husband had lost his first wife the year before they had married. James had pushed her to marry long before a year was up, and she had dragged her feet until she felt that the wedding would not injure the feelings of their respective children. It had not taken more than a few weeks of marriage for her to feel used, and she secretly harbored the thought that what her new husband wanted in a wife was someone to clean up after him. He did not really love her.

The history of this negative imprint was illusive. Had Helen built upon a childhood hurt or a young adult imprint, or was this imprint relatively new? Helen decided that it was new and that Angie had inadvertently torn the scab from the wound of that new negative imprint by revealing during her rant that Mr. Hertzler was a recent widower, and his surprise date with her was to be his inaugural one since his wife had passed. Unfortunately, Angie had also added that Mr. Hertzler wanted very much to marry as soon as possible—completing the trigger thought for Helen.

Helen came to me with her hurts in a bundle, and we worked together to overlay the negative imprint that suggested to her conscious mind that her ex-husband did not love her and neither would Mr. Hertzler.

Execution of the Process

There certainly were similarities between her ex-husband and Helen's nondate of the week before, Mr. Hertzler. For the sake of this lesson I will assume that the negative imprint in her subconscious mind was new and that it was self-imposed. The affirmation that I will use to overlay the negative imprint for this instruction is this: "Love is shown in many ways."

Let's begin with what should now be a trusted and decisive way to change your mind. Since I have chosen the affirmation for this study and because Helen did not use this one but chose another one for herself, I have decided to combine a bit of meditation with the usual instruction to make it more interesting.

- Light a small candle and darken the room you are in.
- Prop a mirror against the wall and place the candle in front of it.

- Sit on the rug in front of them.
- Look into the mirror a little above the flame and repeat the affirmation softly for a few moments: "Love is shown in many ways."
- Avert your eyes to the candle itself and repeat the affirmation once or twice more.
- Close your eyes and repeat the affirmation in your mind.
- Remember that the best way to overlay the negative imprint with the positive affirmation is to patiently repeat the affirmation as many times a day as you are able, because the more you practice the affirmation, the quicker the negative imprint will lose its emotional power over your conscious mind.

Helen was an interesting client because she could usually discover her own negative imprint that had caused an anomaly in the way she lived her daily life. Then she would come to me with her information and we would work together to overlay her imprint. I miss the intelligent way she worked with her subconscious mind in order to keep her conscious mind healthy. I am full of hope that you will come to the place in your heart and mind where you can do the same.

Classic Lines

The classic lines to reflect upon concerning the exercise "Helen and Her Second Marriage" are these simple but profound thoughts: "All experience is a bridge to build upon" (written by Henry Brooks Adams in the year 1907).

Alfred Lord Tennyson wrote prior to that date in 1842 in his book *Ulysses*:

> I am part of all I have met;
> Yet all experience is an arch where through
> Gleams that untraveled world, whose margin fades
> For ever and for ever when I move.

Epilogue

A Chinese philosopher, Chuang Tzu, wrote down this thought three hundred years before the birth of Christ: "The mind of the perfect man is like a mirror. It does not lean forward or backward in response to things. It responds to things but conceals nothing of its own. Therefore it is able to deal with things with out injury to its reality."

An Elegant Echo is the third and final book of simple philosophy concerning the changing of one's mind. The initial book written was *The Joy Reminder*, and the second was *Inside the Honey Walls*. These three books form a set of instructions for you to use to change your mind-set from negative to positive and facilitate the life you were meant to enjoy.

The three mind tools that I chose to write about—affirmation, automatic writing, and meditation—are those that I have personally used since I was a very young girl. They have become part of who I am, and I have logically used them to subdue the negative emotion brought about by a life filled with abuse. But even though the abuse has been a factor in my life, there is no longer negative, hurtful emotion attached to it. You can also face the facts, whatever they may be. Drop those painful stories about them—for that is what you must do first—and use one or all of the mind tools that I have found to be so useful. I am convinced that anyone who has been in my situation can attain an emotionally sound mind by using the tools I have extended to you in my writings.

Each of my three books was written to you, the beginning philosopher, so that your life, although not a smooth one, may contain so much joy in it that just walking into a room full of people will cause the whole room to light up. It can happen—and it will happen for you.

I am extending a lifetime invitation to you to contact me at cjsartco@aol.com with your questions and comments. I welcome all of them.

So, dear readers, until our minds meet again, I send you my blessings as you continue to live your best life. C. J.